HAVE SEX WITH SUCCESS:

Play The Money Game To Win!

Carlyne Edwards

http://sexwithsuccess.com

Dedicated

A beginner guide to investing is an accessible guide to growing your money and assets in a smart way. Whether your intention or dreams are protecting your assets in a turbulent market or creating wealth and abundance, so that you can retire rich, this book is for you. The book includes time-tested advice, updates to investing and strategies that reflect changing market conditions. This resource will serve you as a guide on all aspects of the topics, including how to think positive, passive income, develop and manage real estate, online businesses, etc. This book will help ease your investing confidently for personal finances, investing successfully the smart and easy way.

This Book is dedicated to my Husband and two kids Flint, Najanni and Imani Edwards. You are my inspiration for everything I do, and every decision I make.

Disclaimer:

The information contained in this book is for informational purposes only.

I am not a lawyer or an accountant. Any legal or financial advice I give is my opinion based on my own experience. You should always seek the advice of a professional before acting on something I have published or recommended. Any amount of earnings disclosed in this book should not be considered average.

Please understand there are some links contained in this book I may benefit from financially.

The material in this book may include information, products or services by third parties. Third Party Materials comprise of the products and opinions expressed by their owners. As such, I do not assume responsibility or liability for any Third Party material or opinions.

The publication of such Third Party Materials does not constitute my guarantee of any information, instruction, opinion, products or services contained within the Third Party Material. The use of recommended Third Party Material does not guarantee any success and or earnings related to you or your business. Publication of such Third Party Material is simply a recommendation and an expression of my own opinion of the material.

No part of this publication shall be reproduced, transmitted, or sold in whole or in part in any form, without the prior written consent of the author. All trademarks and registered trademarks appearing in this book are the property of their respective owners.

Users of this book are advised to do their own due diligence when it comes to making business decisions and all information, products, services that have been provided should be independently verified by your own qualified professionals. By reading this book, you agree that myself and my company is not responsible for the success or failure of your business decisions relating to any information presented in this book.

HAVE SEX WITH SUCCESS:

Play The Money Game To Win!

"Money is Freedom and makes life more enjoyable..."

Table of Contents

Introduction

Speaking from my own experience, none of the concepts and insights I share is right or wrong. They simply reflect my own results. I believe if you use the principles you learn in this book, you will totally transform your life.

Don't just read this book, study it and take action. Then, try some of the strategies out for yourself. Whatever works for you, keep doing it. This book will help fulfill your dreams and you will achieve success.

I know you read other books and learned about other rich systems in real estate or business. But what happened? Most people get a short blast of energy, and then, it's back to the same things.

If your thoughts are not set for success, nothing you can learn nothing you can know, and nothing you can do. This will make much of a difference.

Change your non-supportive ways of thinking, so you think—and succeed—just as rich people do. You will learn step-by-step strategies for increasing your income and building wealth.

We are conditioned to think and act a certain way when it comes to money. There are differences between how the rich, middle-class, and poor people think. I will provide actions to change your attitudes and financial life.

What is my experience?

Like many of you, I had a lot of dreams of being successful, but it was not easy. I read all the books, listened to tapes, and went to seminars. I really, really, really wanted to be successful. I don't know whether it was for my family, the life style, money, the freedom or the sense of achievement. I was obsessed with becoming successful or rich, ever since I went to the Rich Dad Poor Dad seminars.

During my twenties, living in Brooklyn, New York I went to a real estate seminar costing about $40k that I borrowed from my Visa card. I had just had a baby and purchased a brand new car and a $3,500 a month mortgage payment. Things were tight. With a debt this big ($40K), I worked my butt off, but kept coming up short. However, I saw lots of potential.

My husband and I decided to move to Florida. Feeling we would definitely accomplish a lot more with the real estate business then we could in New York where properties are so expenses. But with 2 small kids and leaving our jobs, no family to help, it was a real struggle. The only income we had was from our home we rented out.

I was persistent and determined. I never gave up. I was making offers on properties without knowing where the money was coming from. After seven months things began to look better, I made an offer on a property where the seller owned the house free and clear (no mortgage). I did not have go to the bank, the seller would carry a mortgage. From that point on things was getting better. *"Set your mind on a definite goal and observe how quickly the world stands aside to let you pass"* Napoleon Hill. That is what happened!

More important, I don't sit all day and watch TV or socialize on the phone with nonsense. I read a lot of positive books, tapes and go to seminars. These things help me learn several powerful techniques and strategies to actually recondition my mind so I will think in the same way the rich people do.

Finally, I learned in many ways, my mind was my biggest obstacle to success. I chose not to entertain thoughts that did not empower me toward my vision of wealth. I used every one of the principles you are going to learn in this book.

How to Play the money game to win!—how to think rich to get rich! How your old ways of thinking and acting have gotten you exactly where you are right now. If you want success, you have to be willing to let go of some of your old ways of thinking and be able to adopt new ones. The results will eventually speak for themselves.

Ask yourself these questions. Who am I? How do I think? What are my beliefs? What are my habits? How do I feel about myself? How well do I relate to others? How can I help my family and friends? Do I feel I deserve wealth and success? What is my ability to act in spite of fear, in spite of worry, in spite of inconvenience, in spite of discomfort? Can I act when I am not in mood? The fact is your character, your way of thinking, and your beliefs are a critical part of what determines the level of your success.

Chapter 1

The Power of Positive Thinking...

"Whether you believe you can or you can't, you're right." - Henry Ford

Positive Thinking has helped many men and women around the world to achieve fulfillment and success in their lives. Positive thinking is considered to be a mental and emotional attitude, focusing on the right side of life and expecting positive outcomes from anything. A person, who thinks positively,

always anticipates happiness, health and success, believing he/she can overcome any obstacle or difficulty. However, the saddest thing is positive thinking is not accepted by everyone. Some people do not assume or accept the effectiveness of positive thinking. They just consider it nonsense or something not important.

This subject is really gaining popularity these days. To think positively in your everyday life, you need more than just knowing about its existence. You must adopt positive thinking in everything you do. Positive thinking should become your lifestyle. With a positive attitude we always have pleasant and happy feelings. Due to this we feel brighter and full of energy. If you are happy during each day of your life, it also affects your health. You become healthier and stronger. Your voice is more powerful, your eyes shine, and with all your appearance you show you are happy. Both positive and negative thinking are contagious.

We affect and are affected by the people we meet during the day. All this happens instinctively, on a subconscious level, through words, thoughts and feelings. Have you ever wondered why people like to be around positive and happy people and try to avoid negative ones? This is the answer; happy and positive people radiate happiness, brightness and calmness, while negative people – only radiate depression, melancholy and anger. Negative thoughts and words create unhappy feelings and behavior. All this gives way to failure, frustration and vexation.

What negative thoughts do to the brain

Imagine you are walking in the forest and suddenly a bear steps onto your path. At that moment your brain produces negative emotions, in this case - fear. It is found that negative emotions influence your brain in a very bad way, inducing it to some specific actions. When, for example, the bear on your path approaches you, you run, the rest does not matter for you, especially for your brain. You focus on the bear running after you, and fear enslaves you. In short, negative thoughts narrow your mind, focusing it on fear or any other negative thought. You may have other options for being rescued, for example, to climb the tree or grab a stick, at that very moment you are not able to think about any rational outcome, because your brain is vanquished. Of course, it is a useful and important instinct trying to save your life, but now, in our modern society we should not worry about meeting a bear in the wilderness, however, our brain is still programmed to respond to negative emotions in the same way, by narrowing our mind and focusing on fear, anger, depression, etc.

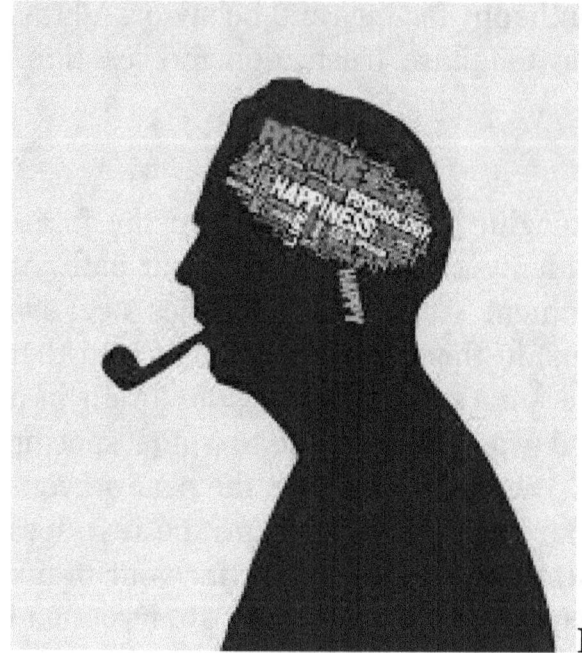

In each case, your brain closes off from the outside world and focuses on the negative emotions. Thus, negative emotions prevent your brain from seeing the other right options and choices that may be found in your surroundings. This is how negative thinking is interfering with the brain.

What positive thoughts do to your brain

The impacts of the positive emotions and thoughts on our brain have been tested many times, and each time the survey showed thinking positive is the best way out from the situation. Barbara L. Fredrickson has carried out several tests on this issue. During one experiment, she divided her research subjects (people) into five groups and showed each group different film clips.

The first two groups were shown clips, which created positive emotions. **Group 1** saw pictures showing joy, and **Group 2** saw images eradiating a feeling of contentment. **Group 3** was the control group. They saw images producing no significant emotion.

The last two groups were shown pictures, expressing negative emotions, **Group 4** was shown images creating an atmosphere of fear, while **Group 5** saw images expressing anger.

Then, each participant was given a piece of paper with 20 blank lines and asked to write what they would do in each situation they were shown. Participants, who were shown pictures full of fear and anger, wrote few responses or way outs from the situations, while the people, who saw pictures showing contentment and joy, wrote down a significantly higher number of actions they would like to do. They gave an even higher number of actions than the control group members did.

In other words, positive thinking is infusing the brain in the most helpful and reasonable way. If you are exercising such emotions like contentment, happiness, brightness and love, you will see more possibilities in your life.

3 things that will increase your positive thinking in your everyday life

What can you do to increase positive emotions and take advantage of them every day? Here are 3 very important steps to do on a daily or weekly basis, in order to widen your mind and think positive.

Meditation. During recent years, research has shown that people who meditate daily, exercise more positive emotions than those who do not. In addition, people who meditate develop long-term skills. People, who have a meditation experience of at least 3 months, can display increased mindfulness, social support, and decreased illnesses. It is not time consuming or a hard thing to do. Just make time each day to meditate, you will see how it is helping.

2. Writing. The Journal of Research in Personality has carried out a survey, examining a group of 90 undergraduate students, who were split into two groups. The first group wrote about a positive experience each day for a three day period. The second group wrote about a control topic. Three months later, the students, who wrote about positive experiences, were happier and had higher mood levels; fewer among them visited the health centers, etc. If you have some time to write, then do it in a positive way, write about something good happening to you. Keep a dairy, but do not complain about your life every day. Just try to remember and see only good things.

3. Engage yourself with new activities. When was the last time you took some time to do something new or extraordinary or simply to play a game? Try to have some positive emotions each day. Try to have at least an hour for you just to explore and experiment something new. Have fun! That is really too important.

Chapter 2:

How the rich think differently from the poor and middle class about money

Since the very beginning people have been split between classes or groups. Ever since the money, the accommodations, and the work have invaded our lives; there were conflicting classes in our society. The split is happening on its own, instinctively. There are three main classes in any society:

1.   The rich

2.   The middle class and,

3.   The poor

Due to varied status and welfare differences, there occur many divergences between the people belonging to different groups. Let's go a bit deeper and explore what are the main differences among the rich, the middle class and the poor.

How the rich approach work and money

Rich people do not work for money to be spent on things, hypothecs or liabilities. They use their money to buy or create assets to pay for those liabilities. This way they keep their money, do not spend it, but still enjoy their lives. They really work some times, but only to create or build assets. They do anything to put their money in action. They hire other people; leverage their time to make them work for them. Most of all rich people spend their time on their luxurious leisure time, having everything of the best quality.

How the poor and middle class approach work and money

Poor and middle class people generally spend their time working for money, earning their living. They earn money and spend it on the things they want. They think over and over again on "how to make some more money." These people have a lot of bills, hypothecs or loans to pay, and things to buy. They want to be paid for their time, in order to pay bills, and buy food and clothes. Here are some examples or contrast between the rich and the poor.

- Rich people say: "I make my own life." - Poor people believe: "Life happens to me."
- Rich people play the money game to win. - Poor people play the money game not to lose.
- Rich people generally think big. - Poor people think small.
- Rich people take into consideration the opportunities. - Poor people focus on the obstacles only.
- Rich people are associated with successful people. - Poor people are associated with unsuccessful ones.
- Rich people are considered to be bigger than their problems. - Poor people are thought to always be smaller than their problems.
- Rich people think "both". - Poor people think "either/or".

- Rich people have their money work hard FOR THEM. - Poor people work hard for THEIR MONEY.
- Rich people act in spite of fear. - Poor people let fear enslave them.

So, now let's look into the differences between the rich and the middle class;

- Rich people think long-term. - The middle class thinks short-term.
- Rich people talk about ideas. - The middle class talks about things and people.
- Rich people welcome changes. - The middle class is afraid of changes.
- Rich people take a calculated risk. - The middle class fears taking risks.
- Rich people expect profit. - The middle class expects wages.
- Rich people think they should be generous. - The middle class thinks it is not able to afford it.
- Rich people have many income sources. - The middle class has only one or two.
- Rich people ask themselves encouraging questions. - The middle class asks discouraging ones.

Of course, there can be exceptions; however, all in all this is the picture. These are the main differences between the classes. Poor and Middle class pay everyone else first, then save or invest what's left over. One thing that all millionaires have in common is they are good at managing their money. Rich people aren't any smarter, they have better money management habits. Managing money doesn't restrict freedom, it promotes freedom.

How the poor, the middle class and the rich spend their money

NPR's Planet Money has recently posted an infographic showing the differences between the poor, the middle class and the rich spend money. The graph shows everyone's rent is really high, also each class spends a lot on transportation and gasoline, food, healthcare, and insurance, as well. The rich succeed at saving for retirement. The conditions are the worst for the poor.

How The Poor, The Middle Class And The Rich Spend Their Money

Type of Spending	Household Income $15,000–$19,999	$50,000–$69,999	Above $150,000
Food At Home	10.2%	7.7%	5.4%
Food At Restaurants, Etc.	4.7%	5.4%	5.4%
Housing	40.3%	34.9%	32.3%
Utilities	11.1%	8.2%	4.8%
Clothes & Shoes	3.6%	3.2%	3.7%
Transportation & Gasoline	20.4%	21.3%	15.5%
Health Care & Health Insurance	8.2%	7.1%	4.5%
Entertainment	4.8%	5.1%	5.7%

Chapter 3:

Escape the 9-5 rat race

Do not waste your precious time

Just imagine waking up on a Monday morning and not going to your usual rate race, known as a JOB. Are you excited now? Then, let's go and explore something which will amaze and inspire you. I bet you dream of working 2-3 hours a day on your laptop from your balcony. This sounds a bit unrealistic, but I can make you sure it can work. You are able to make this come true, if you just believe in what you do and have courage and patience. There is not a secret plan or program; this can be carried out by anyone.

Being able to escape your 9-5 job is not a matter of financial readiness, but a mental one. The finance is just an excuse for many. So, now are you ready to break free from your dull and severe rat race? Are you ready to make your own schedule, to be your own boss, choose from where to work and when to have rest?

You are not an employee any more

It is not the financial dependence or payment check preventing you from quitting a job and starting your own business or work remotely. That is your fear of uncertainty and doubt. If you overcome them, you will be able to start something new. From early childhood we are taught to work, earn money and pay bills. We are trained to put on ties, clock in, say "yes sir" to the boss and work from 9AM-5PM. Let's break these stereotypes. Most people are stuck in the WANT phase and do not move to the DO phase. Do not be one of them.

The employee believes that in order to succeed, He/she must always impress the boss. He/she believes working harder and faster is a way to get a raise or promotion. It's time you stopped thinking like that. Tell yourself you are capable of gathering money on a daily basis for your living without taking part in that awful rat race. You have valuable skills and knowledge that can be devoted to money-making products and services. For example, now your company pays you $15 per hour for you skills and knowledge, but you are not so satisfied by that money. If you start working on your own you can increase that amount. What you can do well is worth a lot more than your current company is willing to pay for. You can be far more successful on your own. You can take full responsibility for what you are doing, if you start working on your own. You are the boss here. Instead of thinking of yourself as "just an employee", think of yourself as an independent person, who can earn his living by themselves.

Everybody fears being homeless or bankrupt if they quit their job. Instead of thinking negatively, give a chance to the right decision. Imagine the job quitting can have many positive outcomes, e.g. a higher income, the ability to work from anywhere in the world, spending more time with family and friends, better health, satisfaction from what you do.

It is not so easy to gather income that will allow you to quit your current job, which you do not like. However, think that you can start from small and then, grow during some time. When it comes to earning your living on your own, you either can provide a service or sell a product.

As everywhere and in everything in this life, there are both advantages and drawbacks in both, you can see them listed below.

Option 1 – You can make money providing a service

This may seem the easiest way to have income – providing a service.

The advantage of Providing a service is you can have an easy start. If you have great skills and knowledge, you just need to market yourself. You can be a freelancer, or a virtual assistant. This will give you opportunities to work remotely. You can state your own working hours, your working limits, your hourly payment, etc.

The drawback of a service-based income strategy is you are the one who creates the job for yourself. The ability to earn money depends directly on your abilities and availability to work. If you are sick or injured and you need a vacation, you will not get paid for it. It is highly recommended you think of your service-based business as a short-term strategy for leaving your job.

Option 2 – You can make money selling a product The other income option can be selling products.

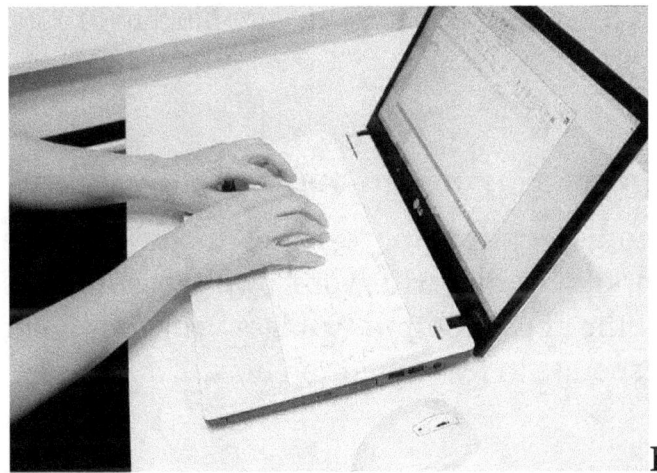

It does not matter whether you are selling your own product or somebody else's, it can be considered as a generating option. It usually does not take much time to create or sell the product.

The advantages of selling a product are you can market it online or sell to buyers, who sell the product for you.

However, the great disadvantage lies in the idea that a large initial investment in a new product is extremely risky. But, you can turn to another idea – that is selling somebody else's product. Can you consider it as a good option?

The answer is - not always! I think you have heard about Pyramid Schemes. These "businesses" require an upfront investment, monthly product purchases, subscription fees, etc. This option is usually very hard to bring to life.

Option 3– You can make money online

Another option for earning money can be working online with your own website. This is the best option, unless you are not desperate to leave your job now.

Ther e are many advantages of creating a website that generates income online. First of all, your website is generating money whether you are working on it or not. This is not a joke! You can earn money even while sleeping. The other advantage is you have a global reach, not just your family, friends and locals. With the website, you can create information products for no money upfront and sell them for almost pure profit. You can even launch a website and generate money without having an information product to sell. It is really difficult to earn a living only with affiliate marketing. Very few people can manage this. If you really want to start this, you can use of Google AdSense; this will really help you start getting income from your website. http://sexwithsuccess.com

Creating many sources of income

It is important you have several sources for generating income, if you are deciding to leave your current job. It is recommended you have income through online sources. First of all, let's understand the necessity of having multiple income streams. Employees accept only one income source - that is the paycheck. However, this paycheck may be cut off, if your boss does not need your work anymore. The results will be awful; many are experiencing this, especially these days.

So, how to create multiple streams of income? You can create websites over time. However, a better idea would be to create one website and place carefully selected affiliate ads for products that are specifically targeted to your readers. This can be source number 1. You can place paid advertising on your website. This is source number 2. You can create e-Books, audios or video products to be sold. This is source number 3. If you are active on your website, your content increases and your readers grow in number. You can create a mailing list and send a newsletter with target product promos in them. This is source number 4. So, this way the list of sources can be prolonged. Just try to think creatively and look at things from different angles.

Some suggestions for understanding the right time to leave a job

So, everything written above will help you make your life without the 9-5 rat race, but how to understand you do not need your current job anymore? How to choose the right time?

1.   The day you look in the mirror and ask yourself whether you are happy with your current job and the answer is "no."

2.   The day you would rather work as a slave when there it is 90+ degrees, than go to work.

3.   You understand you have skills you can cash in on, and you really seek change.

4.   You have a website or two and a mentor, guiding you through the steps necessary to make it work.

These are the main reasons why you must stop doing something you do not like. You have only one life, so start doing something that is close to your heart. Do not fear changes.

Chapter 4:

Don't work for money, have your money work for you.

It is crucial to understand how to succeed with having money work for you. There are a lot of people who fail here. So, what should you do to make your cash work for you?

First of all, make sure you have the following list and can follow the guidelines:

- You have a budget. Of course, this is the most important part.

- You are saving for retirement. Before thinking about what to do with your money, consider how much you will need in retirement, save as much as possible.

- You have paid off all your debt. This is not about credit cards; this is about all the debts you have, e.g. car loans, mortgages, student loans, etc. You have an emergency fund. It's very important.

Now, let's move on to some guidelines to be followed in order to make your money work for you.

1. **Start saving.** This is the easiest part. Start to save some amount from your paycheck in a savings or investment account. Your money cannot work for you, if you do not put some aside. PAY YOURSELF FISRT! Before you pay any bills, put 10% in a saving.

2. **Savings snowball.** When your money starts to generate returns, that amount of money will be added to your savings and get its own returns. If you do not spend the income from your investments, the extra money will become much bigger.

3. **Money works 24/7**. Even if you leave your money in the account, it will work for you. The long term trajectory is always up, because the global economy is always growing. You get paid even if you don't do any work. If you do not raid the accounts, your money will work for you.

4. **You have to pay fees, too**. There can be cases when having money costs money. You may need a financial adviser in an actively managed mutual fund. On the whole, you can minimize the fees by investing yourself making use of low cost index funds. Pay attention to all expenses.

5. **Have a passive income stream.** Our invested or saved money can become a source of passive income. You can make long term investments with your saving, and this amount will constantly grow. The key point here is to understand how equity markets work. You should also develop a long term game plan, so as not to panic when there is tough times.

Getting money to work for us is easier than many think. If you make an effort to manage your investments, you will be able to invest even more efficiently and effectively. Just find an alternative and easier way for you to have your money work for you.

What is Capital One 360®?

Capital One 360 is an online bank, which helps you save time and money, wherever you are and whatever your banking needs are.

Capital One 360 goes where you go. It serves its customers 24/7. It is possible to reach it online and on mobile devices.

What does Capital 360 do?

1. **Saves you money** – There are checking and savings accounts, which are fee-free. There also are gadgets like *My Savings Goals* to help customers move up the savings path.

2. **Saves you time** – There is a tool like *CheckMateSM* mobile check deposit and also *Automatic Savings Plan,* which helps save time and money in customer's bank accounts.

With 360 checking, each customer is free to roam. There are no hidden fees or minimums as you earn interest on your everyday money. It offers free MasterCard® Debit Card for all purchases. Capital 360 makes it easier to pay bills, send cash to family and friends, etc.

Chapter 5:

Succeeding in investing

Introduction to investing "Scared money, don't make money" by Bilzerian. You must spend money to make money.

Have you ever thought how rich people got their wealth and kept it growing? Do you dream of becoming rich? I bet you do! Do you know from where to start, even if you do not have much money? The right answer can be found here. Just be careful and attentive.

The world of finance can be extremely intimidating; however, business, investing and finance will not seem so complicated once you know some nuances.

However, it should be mentioned investing is not a get-rich-quick plan. Taking control over your finances takes much work, time, devotion and commitment. The rewards will outweigh the required effort. In contrast to spreading belief, you will not need to let banks or investment professionals push your money in directions you barely understand. You can and should be your own boss and professional investor, just have some time and be curious.

Not counting your character, lifestyle or interests, you will find help here, to start your own investments.

In the dictionary you will find the following definition for the word *'investing'- the act of committing money or capital to an endeavor with the expectation of obtaining an additional income or profit.*

It is really simple, actually it means putting your money to work for you.

We have grown up thinking we can earn money by working. Most of us think like that. But it is not the only option for making money. If you think that only by working you will get enough profit you will fail, because you are not a robot who works for days without getting any rest. Also, no one will let you work nonstop, as there are certain hours during which you can work. So, this is a big minus.

Thus, while you are working, sleeping, reading the paper or having leisure time, you can earn money elsewhere. There are many different ways you can go about making an investment. Putting money into stocks, mutual funds, bonds or real estate are types of investing; even you can start your own business. The reality is, it does not matter what option you choose you just need to invest your money and to earn additional money. This sounds easy; however, it will become easy, only when you understand all the nuances involved.

What investing is not

Many people think investing is gambling. However, it is not. Gambling is putting money at risk by betting on an uncertain outcome. This confusion, of course, comes from the wrong way people understand investing. For instance, true investing cannot happen without some action on your part. A "real" investor will not just throw his/her money at random. There should be some analysis, thinking, etc. Yes, you can still be at risk, but you do not just hope for luck only.

Why to invest?

Everybody wants more money. Even if you have billions, you will want to double or triple that money. We are human; that is our nature. It is easy. People invest because they want to increase their personal income, freedom, security and the ability to afford the things they want to have. Freedom to live life on your own terms.

Nowadays, investing has become more of a necessity. Even if you work and get your paycheck, that cannot be enough for our current reality. So, investing can be considered to be a good alternative or another source of income.

Tips on successful investing

It is never too early to start investing. If you want to succeed, you must follow some tips. Here they are:

1. Get acquainted with investment vehicles

Step 1

Have you ever heard about stocks? My guess is yes. However, people often have very wrong understandings of them. A stock is an ownership share in a public company.

When you buy stock in a company, you are making yourself part-owner of that company. If the company fails, the stock will lose its value, if the company succeeds, so do you. The value of stocks comes from public perception of its worth. The stock price depends on what people think about its worth.

Stock prices go up when more people want to buy them, and they decrease when more people want to sell them.

Step 2

The other vehicle is bonds. Bonds are issuances of debt. If you buy a bond, you essentially lend entity money, called the principal. The entity agrees to pay you back the principal, when the life of the loan is up, plus yearly interest.

The longer the life of the bond, the higher the interest rate is. You can witness here that the higher the risk, the larger the return will be.

Step 3

The commodities market is another opportunity for investing. A commodity is an item that satisfies wants and needs, like pork belly, coffee beans, or electricity. The thing is often valuable, because people need and use it.

People often trade commodities by buying and selling "futures." It seems complex, but it is simple. A future is simply an agreement to buy or sell a commodity at a certain price in the future.

Step 4

Investing in real estate is another vehicle. It can be both a risky and lucrative proposition at the same time. You have to buy right! You can buy a house, rent or lease option it out. You can also flip houses, meaning buy a house which need renovation, fix it up, and sell it as quickly as possible (cash flow). Wholesaling properties in a nut shell puts property (normally distressed property) under contract and assigns or resells the property to another investor. This can happen without using your own money. This is one of my favorite strategies. Owner financing meaning, the person who sells the real estate agrees to take payment over time for the purchase price of that property. For example, if you buy a house from a seller and the seller agrees that you can pay $1,000 per month over 30 years, this would be owner financing, also called seller financing. I love real estate, you have so many options. Buying real estate properties subject to etc.

2. Mastering investment basics

Step 1

First of all, consider buying undervalued assets. If you want to buy stocks or other assets, you must buy them when they are cheap and sell them at a higher price.

How to understand the stock is undervalued? Take the company and explore its projected revenue, its P/E ratio, etc. Use your critical thinking skills, in order to understand whether the stock is undervalued or not.

Step 2

Invest in companies, you understand. It is a big mistake to invest in something you don't know anything about. Invest in companies and industries you know, as you are more likely to understand revenue models and future success.

Step 3

It is too easy to follow the crowd when investing. Never do that. When you buy a stock everyone else has bought, you are buying something already worth less than what its price is. When you sell a stock everyone else is selling, you are selling something, which may be worth more than its price.

Step 4

Diversify your portfolio. It is a very crucial point in investing, which will mitigate your risks. If you invest $5 in 20 different companies, each company could go broke, so you lose, if you invest $100 in one company, the risks are high for a loss, as there is only one company. Try to invest in different types of assets.

Step 5

Choose stable investments and hang on to them for a long time. Each time you invest in something, the broker takes his amount commission for connecting you with another seller or buyer. If you invest in one company for a long time, you will pay just once.

3. Making the most of your money

Step 1

Think about using the services of a financial planner or adviser. However, most of the advisers work with portfolios of $100,000, $200,000 or larger. So, your portfolio should be well-established. But if you are a newbie, there will be advisers to work with smaller investments. Financial planners are professional and they can help you with something you do not understand or do not know a way out. They want you to succeed, as the more money you have in the end, the more money they can earn from it.

Step 2

You can also get an investment broker. The broker is a person, who executes trades for you. It will be easier for you to have someone to help you. There are different kinds of brokerage services available.

Step 3

It is important to know the players in the game. It is really great to be an independent investor, though it will be helpful to know who is playing the game with you. As they say 'Keep your friends close and your enemies closer.'

Step 4

Reexamine your investment strategies and targets. The conditions of the market change so quickly, you must always keep up with them.

Be smart, think about each detail and you will succeed.

Chapter 6:

BUSINESS AND INVESTMENT TAXES

Business taxes

Once you become a business owner, you are responsible for making tax payments, which you did not have as an employee. May be you did not know, but your employer was transmitting those taxes by withdrawing them from your paycheck and sending them to the government. So, here you will be introduced to the taxes you are required to pay once you have your own business.

Estimated taxes

As you are a business owner, you should put aside some amount of money gathered from your clients. Your clients, of course, will not take any taxes out of their checks to you. You should make tax payments, if you expect to have at least $1,000 in tax for the year after subtracting any tax credits. The estimated tax payments consist of yearly amounts, which are equal to 100% of what you had in the previous tax year or sometimes, 90% of what you expect to have in the current tax year.

When your earnings for the year are less than or similar to what you expect to earn your first year in business, you can pay 100% of your previous year's tax for your current year's estimated tax payments. This is a way out.

You need to submit your estimated federal tax payments along with a corresponding IRS voucher four times a year. You can sign up for the (EFTPS) Electronic Federal Tax Payment System, which will allow you to make electronic payments. If you are self-employed, be sure to calculate what you will owe in advance and keep some amount in your business bank account, in case the bill is higher than you expected. If there is income tax in your state, then you should go through a similar procedure and pay state tax.

Self-Employment tax

There is no separate tax on the self-employed. Self-employment tax contains Medicare and Social Security payments. If you are an employee, then 6.2% of your paycheck is withheld for Social Security and 1.65% - for Medicare.

If you are self-employed, you are the employer, so you match those amounts. So, this matching portion is self-employment tax. Totally, you pay 15.3% in Social Security and Medicare taxes on 92.35% of your net earnings.

Self-employment tax is not paid quarterly, it is submitted as a lump sum with your annual tax return using IRS schedule *SE*, Self-Employment Tax. You are required to pay self-employment tax in April.

Business tax deductions

A small business owner has some duties, like deducting business expenses from taxable income. Let's imagine your marginal tax bracket is 25%. This means that any income you earn above the minimum income limit set by the IRS is taxed at 25%.

Tax deductions absolutely do not make your business purchases free. Tax deductions help in those cases, when you really do need some items to buy for your business.

Here are some tax deductions types you should be aware of - health insurance premiums, home office costs, entertainment, internet, meals, phone, business travel, loan interests, education costs and self-employed retirement plan contributions.

Payroll taxes

Once you hire an employee or structure your business as a C Corporation, making you an employee, your tax situation becomes more complex. Due to this, you will need to withhold federal and state income taxes and FICA (Social Security and Medicare) taxes, on behalf of all the employees. All this will make you pass through additional paperwork and even make more frequent tax payments using IRS form 941, Employer's Quarterly Federal Tax Return, as well as, the equivalent state form. Once your tax liability is high enough, you will have to pay monthly or semiweekly instead of quarterly.

If you have employees, you may be made to pay state unemployment insurance.

Hiring an accountant

If this tax stuff has totally confused you, you can hire a helping hand to help. Most people are not even able to prepare their personal tax returns, let alone the more compound returns required from you, if you have a business. If you do not understand the requirements and cannot correctly prepare returns and calculate payments, it is worth spending some money and hiring an accountant. An accountant's expertise will also help you avoid tax penalties.

Even if you hire an accountant, you still will have to keep records.

Investment tax basics

It is really too important for all investors to understand what the government will take in different types of investments Taxes vary based on the type or investment.

Tax on dividends

Companies pay dividends from after-tax profits. This can mean the taxman has already taken a cut. That is why shareholders get a break - a preferential tax rate of 15% on qualified dividends, if the company is based in a country that has a double-taxation treaty acceptable to the IRS. Non-qualified dividends, paid by other foreign companies receiving non-qualified income are taxed at regular income tax rates, which are generally higher. However, in 2013, there was a sliding scale up to 39.6%, plus an additional 3.8% surtax for high income taxpayers ($200,000 for singles, $250,000 for married couples). Shareholders benefit from the preferential tax rate only if they have held shares for at least 61 days during the 121-day period beginning 60 days before the dividend date.

Tax on interests

The federal government treats most interest as ordinary income, which are taxed at whatever marginal rate the investor pays. Even though the investors do not receive any cash until maturity, they must pay taxes on the annual interest. Investors should check the federal tax status of any municipal bond before they buy.

Tax losses and wash sales

Investors may offset capital gains against capital losses realized either in the same tax year or carried forward from previous years. Individuals may deduct up to $3,000 of net capital losses against other taxable income each year. Investors can minimize their capital gains tax liability by getting tax losses.

The IRS treats the sale and repurchase of a "substantially identical" security within 30 days as a "wash sale", for which the capital loss is disallowed in the current tax year. The loss increases the tax basis of the new position, deferring the tax consequence until the stock is sold in a transaction that isn't a wash sale.

Real Estate investment trust taxes

Real estate investment trusts (REITs) offer tax-efficient exposure to the real estate market. Investors here have to pay ordinary income tax on their dividends and on shares bought and sold. However, REIT shares are taxed only after they earn back that part of the investment used to finance real estate purchases and improvements. Consequently, investors may time their tax liability for their REIT shares.

Taxes have a significant impact on the net return to investors. If you really want to succeed in your investment legally, then do not avoid paying taxes.

Chapter 7:

Get rich or Die trying

Right-thinking and creative frames of mind are all preconditions for getting what you want in this life. Persistency is a very important thing in life. Being persistent is a skill that can help you to achieve your aim, get what you really have passion for. Persistency and its application is often the blind line by which successful and unsuccessful people can be distinguished. Giving up too soon is one of the most common reasons why people fail in their endeavor.

The role of persistence in achieving any goal, overcoming any obstacle and getting what you want in interactions with other people is great. It helps in every sphere of human life.

Persistency is a crucial part in business, as well. Being persistent in business will only make it easier to achieve your goals. Business is a field full of unpredictability, so is life. We cannot be sure about the outcome of each activity.

These guidelines will help you understand the importance of persistency and also how it will work with your daily deeds.

Persistence is the key to having a successful business

First of all, in any venture you must have passion, whether it is finding the right schools for your children or wanting to be a successful businessperson or an entrepreneur. You should have a motivation to wake up every morning and accomplish your goal. You must have passion and enthusiasm to go to work every day or just work on yourself to open your own business. Lack of enthusiasm is not a good scenario for your business development.

If you have lost interest, you should just stop and rethink what can help you regain your interest. The last thing you want to do is work for the money only. You should find more than just money to motivate you. If you do not try to be persistent in your business, then you are likely not to have any gain from it. Business can succeed through passion and motivation. Remember, if you are not ready for that, someone else will be instead of you. So, try to work on yourself.

Try to give new strength to clarity. Being clear on your visions and plans will help you avoid a lot of unnecessary trial and error. Not knowing what you want in the future is like driving a car without knowing the address of your destination. You can imagine a journey, how good it can be, but without a clear path it will be really challenging for you.

You can map or set your route, your goals and aims. Many business people succeed by doing that. With the help of this, you know where you are going and how long it will take to get there.

Always keep in mind all the obstacles and elements that may hinder your path, and set aside some alternative paths, which may require a diversion. If you are the business owner, always guide and lead your team through the path you want to see yourself in, during the next several years. The clarity of your business should be set in each member of your team. If the path is too long or complicated, you can break it down into several parts. Make shorter, achievable goals.

For a startup business, there are a lot of obstacles that may hinder your path. The outcome, will be enjoyable, but the process is not so easy. Not everyone is a giving person.

This may seem discouraging, and you may also ask yourself why you took this journey in the first place. You may often lose and the bad periods can be long.

However, you can only succeed in business through persistence. Reevaluate your business, your efforts and actions; what is going wrong and what is right? Do not continue anything, until you clear out what is going on. In other words, use your 'side view mirrors' and 'windshield wipers.'

Together with business evaluations and persistence, there is something as important as these two; that is commitment. You need to be committed in everything you do. If you do not have commitment, you will both physically and mentally withdraw from any task you do. If you have invested a lot of time and money into your business, you cannot give up on it. No matter what is going on right now, you must stay committed to what you do. You need to have vast control and authority, and be committed and well organized, in order to succeed.

So, in conclusion it should be stated, for a successful business startup you need to know what your target is. Also, you need some clarity in your actions, and clear and strong beliefs to achieve your goals

If you have a long path, you can break it down into smaller pieces. You must be a good leader knowing all the strong and weak points of your team members. Know the strengths and weaknesses of your team members and allocate the right tasks based on their strengths.

You should be confident in what you do. Do not be discouraged of every single failure. Be 100% committed to your business and recognize your strengths and weakness. Be persistent! Read the story, Three Feet from Gold by Sharon L. Lechter.Turn Your Obstacles in Opportunities!

Closing

Thank You So Much! I hope you've enjoyed this Book as much as I loved writing it for you. I can't thank you enough for your continued support of HAVE SEX WITH SUCCESS: Play the Money Game to Win and everything I do. I appreciate each and every one of you for taking time out of your day or evening to read this book, and if you have an extra second, I would love to hear what you think about this book. Please leave a nice testimonial and a five star review about the book. A credibility testimonial requires a purchase of the book. Thanks again, and I wish you nothing less than success!

Build Massive Wealth

BE THE BOSS.
DATE A BOSS.
BUILD AN EMPIRE...

"Success in life comes when you simply refuse to give up, with goals so strong that obstacles, failure, and loss only act as motivation."

Say the following affirmation

"I REFUSE TO BE ANYTHING BUT SUCCESSFUL... I WILL SUCCEED PERIOD"

Author: Carlyne Edwards

I am a dedicated mother of two and wife. I love to shop, travel and spend time with my family. I got into real estate after a career in education. Then, after going to a real estate seminar, I became interested in real estate investing. I chose my career in real estate investing, so I could use my skills to educate people and help them make the best real estate decisions possible. Writing this book has allowed me to do this. I take a great deal of pride in my professional expertise and in the level of knowledge I acquired throughout the years. I really believe when we give more than is expected of us, we get much more than we expect or could imagine. I love investing in real estate, buying, selling, rehabbing, etc. My goal is to be known as a valuable resource for anyone, who is thinking of investing to fulfill their dreams and achieving success.

During the past five years I have been blessed with more good fortune than the average person, but I shudder to think where I'd be today, or what I'd be doing if I had not been exposed to the Rich Dad Poor Dad book. I hope this book influences your life for the better. Have a prosperous and blessed life...

http://sexwithsuccess.com

Carlyne Edwards

www.ingramcontent.com/pod-product-compliance
Lightning Source LLC
Chambersburg PA
CBHW070931180526
45168CB00003B/1035